Never Again That Simple

Never Again That Simple

poems by
Susan Lagsdin

☙❧

Methow Press
Twisp, Washington 98556

© 2024 Susan Lagsdin

Published by Methow Press

P.O. Box 1213, Twisp, WA 98856
https://www.methowpress.com

Printed in the United States of America

All rights reserved. No part of this publication may be reproduced, stored in a retrieval system, or transmitted in any form or by any means—for example, electronic, photocopy, or recording—without the prior written permission of the publisher. The only exception is brief quotations in printed reviews.

ISBN 13: 979-8-9913567-0-1

Cover and interior scenic images © Mike Irwin. Used by permission.
Cover graphics design by Greg Wright.

I am pleased to share some scenes and thoughts I've held dear for years. I hope you peruse this book with an occasional wry sigh or a knowing smile—there's very little pain and much pleasure in these pages, and it's all for you.

This collection presents about two percent of the poems I could've, would've, should've written when thoughts collided with me or the perfect words swam into view, but it will suffice. I thank teachers and students who've inspired me, friends who've encouraged me, writing groups who've questioned me, listeners who've buoyed me, and especially Mike, who's always assumed I would do this... someday.

Susan

Contents

I.

Winter Tree	3
Methow Pantoum	4
November	5
Western Dream	6
Real. Pretty.	8
Methow Wind	9
In Country	10
Leaving the Methow: What I Will Miss	12
Terra Firma Eastside	14
Spring Snow	15
June 21	16
February	17
At Porter's Pond	17
Chorus	17
At The Dalles	18
Habitat I: Reminder	19
Habitat II: Renewal	20
Habitat III: Reunion	21

II.

Air Space	25
Postwar Script	26
Sisters	28
Treasures	29

Legacy	30
Vigil	32
Floating	33
Childless	34
When I Try	35
I've Never Asked	36
Cuppa	37
Road Trip	38
Call and Response	39
You Fill Me	40

III.

Patio, Circa 1955	45
Learning the Waters	46
Three Cheers for Fears	47
Old Ways and Nowadays	48
Dreams of Dude String Horses	
I. On the Picket Line	50
II. The Old Campaigner	51
Insomnia	52
The Big Z	53
Everybeach	54
Georgia on My Mind	55
Hey! Don't ever try to tell me	56
Metrical	57
No eating no dogs	58
My Heaven	60
Acknowledgments	63
About the Author	65

I.

The hills and trails of the Methow Valley and the shores of the Columbia River—our shared geography—have shaped my life for decades and found a resting place in my memory.

Winter Tree

Once, a life ago, I knew that to sketch our cottonwood trees
Given pure white paper and black ink
I'd know how to show the ever-complicating swirl
Of twig and leaves and the darkness of branch and limb.

I would imagine the scratch of nib on velum
As the grooves and whorls of comforting ink
Filled in upon themselves
Turning the hazy memory tree a certain black
against a sky of papery white.

But then I looked with a new eye at our tree against a winter sky—
At palest creamy bark crosshatched with cloud-soft grey
The underside of leftover leaves glowing like the bowls of old spoons
The tan lace pillar of trunk catching four o'clock sun straight on.
And the sky looming behind like a melodrama curtain
Deep purple thunderheads darkening the edgeless north.

Not black on white at all.
Never again that simple.

☙❧

Methow Pantoum

(a traditional Malaysian form brought to France in the 19th Century)

I loved the Methow storms in late November
When ragged clouds crept darkly from the west
And after years away I still remember
A jagged line that formed the mountain's crest.

When ragged clouds crept darkly from the west
The snowfall softly covered every field
And a jagged line that formed the mountain's crest
Held up against the sky an iron shield.

And softly snowfall covered every field
When cattle circled tight against the weather.
Held up against the sky an iron shield
The mountains ranged back westward to forever.

While cattle circled tight against the weather
Inside the wood stove glowed into the night.
The mountains ranged back westward to forever
With snowflakes blanketing earth in eerie white.

Inside the woodstove glowed into the night
And after years away I still remember
With snowflakes blanketing earth in eerie white
I loved the Methow storms in late November.

CR8O

November

Pasture grasses are bit cuticle-low to the ground
Pale with frost and loss.
Riverbend trees show darkened remnants of their leaves
Rosehips darken, thistles loll spent against the fence
Uneven ground grows rock hard
And cattle in their flat home fields mourn basso profundo
For the freedom of their summer mountain range.
After circling above to sight late-hibernating mice
A rocketing red-tailed hawk swoops in low.

At home, south windows warm the house by midday
And quarter-rounds of Doug fir are stacked to the woodshed roof.
With the woodstove ticking, low-voiced radio, coffee cup, open book
I give thanks for the coming solitude
For cold and covering snow
And the few suspended months of winter

Where I am unburdened
Secure in the structure that's stood for one hundred years,
Neither prey nor pursuer, neither yearning nor dying.

ଓଃ

Western Dream

(a true life real estate saga)

The seller would finance a contract
With just ten thousand down in cash.
But the hillside was steep, the woods overgrown,
And the gully held decades of trash.
Not the property city folks dream of
When they search for their country retreat—
Their big western dream has a clear running stream
And a ski trail that's right down the street.

Some family once thought it was perfect,
But the work got too hard—they were done.
So the seasons collapsed the small house and the barn,
And the meadow just baked in the sun.
Power and water could be had for a price,
Installed in a matter of weeks,
But the home site, just one, looked straight on to a hill,
Not the river or snow-covered peaks.

I despaired of its sale in my lifetime,
And to show it meant swallowing pride,
But the couple that entered the office that day
Was willing to go for the ride.
A four-wheel-drive trek brought us up to the land,
To the grassy flat spot where I parked.
We examined the buildings and walked up to the edge
To show them the lot lines I'd marked.

Despite the young duo's polite inquiries,
I knew that a sale would be toast.
But I'll give them this, they were nicer than some
And more open-minded than most.
We were turning to leave in a silence I knew
When the wife gave a gasp of surprise.
Her husband and I turned to look to the east
To the bordering property's rise.

Now, I know that this never happens,
And I guess that you'll think I'm a liar
But I swear that I'll always remember that moment with—
Yes, you heard it: my buyer.
The neighbor's few horses had broke loose from their pen
And went for a lark on the hill
(The one visible feature facing this site) and I can remember it still:

In the midmorning sun they were galloping free,
Some colts and some too old to ride.
As they reached the top of the ridge facing us,
They saw people across the divide.
The big chestnut reared, a statue of gold,
With his hooves reaching up to the sky.

That did it—the Dream of the West had come true!
And that couple was ready to buy.

₢₰

Real. Pretty.

The sky was blue. Boy was it blue.
Blue, not quite turquoise like a
Phoenix widow's bracelet,
not quite the blue of that paper-lined
fragment of robin's egg you find on the lawn after a windstorm,
not quite the copper-fed teal of
a high mountain lake at the end of a hike.
But it was very blue.

And snow—all kinds of gray and cream and even breathless white
still hunkered on the shadier slopes.

Earth exposed itself to the south
brown as only the word brown can be,
most trees smudged copper ink drawings,
rosy maroon shrubs about to think of spring
and then—the river! A shining snake, a chameleon,
scales reflecting all the gold and silver of the sun and sky.

But nothing popped the senses
wide open that early morning,
walloped the eyeballs   sizzled the soul
caught the breath deep down at the gut
like driving around the ridge to see
a herd of hot air balloons just unleashed from the valley floor.
Five massive teardrop globes ascended,
each one a silk kaleidoscope of lime, blue, jade and violet
hyped-up primary paintbox colors

taking on nature for the prize of... real pretty.

☙❧

Methow Wind

Methow wind, dropping cold
down rock-faced high Cascades
handpicks and stirs with abandon
first cedar, larch, salal and huckleberry
meandering southeast
shopping for scent
collects bunchgrass, sage, and bitterbrush
plucked from the broadening valley
and lays on the last perfumes:
rosehips and lilacs from homestead yards
fresh cut alfalfa vast and fragrant in the field.

Methow wind waits
until navy blue dark
long after the last copper slant of light
has slipped off Oval Peak
then swoops with pungent armloads
over grassy benches and down dirt roads
hovering in moonlight
a stone's throw from Beaver Creek
then gently slips through my window screen
and like a stealthy lover
brings me a bouquet
of cool sweet smells for dreaming.

༄༅

In Country

The Methow Valley, East Side County Road. 10:20 on a spring night.
Just full dark. Going south past river-bottom ranches
my headlights pick up mailboxes, phone poles,
at-ease sprinkler pipes banked against the fence,
the slurry of gravel shoulder touching ditchweed,
slick tire marks on the asphalt looping around cut-bank curves
and then ahead
the straddling, earnest body of an April fawn
picking his way on petal hooves across the road from left to right.

My lights explode on him.
He freezes, turns to face the car
now fully stopped ten feet away,
idling a cougar's purr, the lights two stunning suns.
Gangly knees turned inward,
the fawn stands paralyzed, mesmerized.

Seconds later, two headlights grow behind him
coming north at full speed, dipping low, homing in
until our stunned tableau springs from the darkness
and with a squeal of brakes the pickup truck
stops.

Immobile, we two drivers point south and north
and the fawn
stunned in blinding headlights
sways uncomprehending back and forth.

In hope I click my headlights off
and one bright heartbeat later
so does the other driver.

Still air, dark sky, tree shapes, the deep bodies of mountains—
suspended in this stillness
we face each other under a dome of darkness
now breathing together, wanting one thing
in finite communion.

The blessing of our darkness sends the fawn, now just a shadow
walking surely step by step
to the west, to the fence, to the field, to the river.

Now we two drivers, who will never know each other's faces,
switch on our headlights, flash them once in thank-you and farewell,
and drive our own ways, south and north
in the Methow Valley, on the East Side County Road
at 10:20 on a spring night.

ଓଃ୪ଠ

Leaving the Methow: What I Will Miss

In Spring:
minute lime green sprouts of cottonwood
unfurling into darker leaves,
balsam bunches on every south slope
the day the ditch starts up,
open moonscape hills sprayed with green velvet.

In Summer:
scent of sage and bitterbrush
on an early morning trek up the hill,
the knee-deep shock of ditch water
to clean gardening legs,
ankles on the porch rail at 5:00 with drink and book in willow shade.

In Autumn:
the first pale turn of leaf
and scent of school and chill and sadness,
the last bales stacked
and morning sprinklers frosted into statues,
the shoulders of McClure Mountain shrugging off the first snowfall.

In Winter:
powder sugar crust of bright new snow
parting from the red shovel,
fuzz and fatness of the horse
with frosted straws of whiskers,
the crack and thud of fir rounds smacked open by the sledge.

I will miss in every season knowing whose truck is where and why and whose dog is trotting on the road and who shouldn't hang around the supermarket lot and whose sister is visiting. Understanding why she has three jobs, why he walks with a limp, why their house is always dark, why the children are shy, why the corn is on the north field this year, why they sold the ranch, why the car is in the shop, why the laughter from the other table, why the new perm and tight jeans, why the package on the steps and why the morning stop at the tavern. Recognizing who is leaning on the pickup talking, who is striding through hip deep alfalfa, who is picking up the bundled mail, who is hauling logs roaring down the highway, who is folding on the shelf a shipment of too-bright sweaters, who is at the power pole balanced on a crane like an acrobat, who is wrapping steaks in plastic and who is running the Chevon card through the little machine and gazing down the highway wishing.

I will miss philosophers, philanderers, and fliers,
sopranos, chefs, and calf ropers.
For all time I will treasure
who you are and who I am
in our delicate ecosystem
and our constant, casual concern
for the minutia of each other's lives.

Mostly I will miss the warm embrace, the known face.

ଔଛ

Terra Firma Eastside

Keep your lullaby-soft terrain and shades of jade
your temperate zone of pewter clouds
curves of greenery, viny woodlots, pastures
masking mudlegged dairy cows and blackberry chaos.
Keep your monotonous moist terrarium.

Give me the ground that deluge scraped
for millennia, made prehistoric shrapnel
where sage and bitterbrush stake out a life
and thin dirt hugs gravel close beneath.

Grant me battle-scarred cliffs above the river
basalt forts guarding tumbled shards
hardrock hills sprayed
with the green veneer
that stands for spring around here.

Keep your damp land of seeping bog.

This terra firma under oath
testifies what's always been beneath our feet
defines the stuff the planet's really made of.

☙

Spring Snow

Cool white sheeting muffles the early crocus
frosting the foothills, powder-brushing the phone lines and shrubs.
An April snowstorm sets our inner clocks awry, with pale evenings
a stark midwinter landscape, blustery sky.

This rogue snowfall
makes closer neighbors of the towhees
who swoop into dry untypical crannies for a meal.
Invited here by warming skies,
they find their worms and seeds buried inches below
beneath a bird's height
of unexpected powder snow.

☙❧

June 21

The first full morning of summer means
tiny ruby slippers of cut strawberries
just found in the neglected rock garden
newly planted daisies languishing in last week's heat
and honeysuckle thriving despite me.

It means fledgling quail scattering laterally
like birdshot through the brush
concerned parents chip-chip-chipping behind
a stiff west wind blustering up whitecaps on the river
cloudplay over the mountains a crazy opera set of cumulus and sky.

Blessedly lacking in seasonal memory
I view this June day through a tipped prism of astonishment.

༶༶༶

February

Pampered suburban lawnscapes
are overmowed tangled khaki mats,
the sodden remnant of last summer's labor.
While in the ditch, emerald grasses
unvalued, untouched
flourish, reaching high.

At Porter's Pond

The island taunts us, almost walkable.
A slick stone path at low tide
becomes dots in deep water by noon.
Waterfowl nest at the edge,
secure in their slight isolation.

Chorus

Denning coyote in the gulch
and far above
the migrant geese
sing the same refrain.
Translation? We own this earth
this sky, this primeval song.

☙❧

At The Dalles

Ancient fishery where salmon leapt glinting through the froth
today Chinook village remnants, thin gray lumber
are shoved sideways by a century of stiff gorge wind,
and the rickety fishing platforms rest empty below the cliff.
Fifty yards away the Shilo Motel Bar and Portage Grill
borders the interstate.

At the back door, near the dumpster,
John Oatman, with waist-long black hair and feather,
red tee-shirt and ragged cutoffs,
hails me in from the path, tells me his story:
Descended from Lapwai and Kamiah elders, breeders of Appaloosas,
he prays to know his spirit brothers at this place.

John smokes his last Marlboro,
sips a Styrofoam coffee the busboy's just sneaked out to him
and offers to sell two items he's stowed close by:
a small basket or a big fish.
If that's not of interest (he makes it simpler) a dollar will do
or even a quarter—if that's all you've got today.

☙❧

Habitat I: Reminder

A swimmer left his shirt behind
jammed into a stump near the river's beach,
disguised by shade and darkened
by a few days' rising and receding waters.
A good shirt—some slick synthetic stuff
heavy and well-stitched
short-sleeved
with jaunty kaleidoscopic checks in white and black.

What to tell the weekend's heedless swimmer?
How to remind him that his bare-chested walk home
left a part of him in the woods?

And how to warn him
that when he returns seeking the shirt
he'll find himself in gently swaying effigy
upon a man-high snag,
pushed carelessly by the wind
a horizontal branch through sleeves
defining his pointy shoulders,
a green-tasseled alder branch for his silly head?

A half-embodied monument to forgetfulness,
a shiny checkered scarecrow not even the blue herons find alarming.

ೞ

Habitat II: Renewal

The irrigation stream's been altered
into a tiny knee-deep pond
easing over a hand-stacked rock dam
that spills water to the river's natural edge,
a haven for the family
(children safely squealing
in the quiet chill of ditchwater)
gathered in dappled pastel shade
that triple-digit day—

Seurat's Sunday in the park
marred only by detritus
they've left beside the pool:
one cigarette pack
a quarter-folded diaper
twisted cans lying rampant
on an empty beer case.

Time and the kindness of strangers will erase
the unmannered litter.
The beach will lie in peace again
and the soft counterpoint
of birdsong, the distant hum of summer bees,
the tender slap of waves upon the shore
will magically mute the distant whine of outboard racers
and the heart-grabbing crash of train coupling
thundering across the river.

☙❧

Habitat III: Reunion

At the river someone's nestled four long branches
lean-to like against a low curved limb
and when I walk by
I wedge a stick or two across the others
resting, notched,
amid the frequent additions of earlier walkers
wielding other twigs and branches.

We're building, sight unseen, not so much a hut
as a suggestion of a hut,
a breath rather than an inspiration.
We keep at our task all winter.

Sometimes footsteps in the crusty earth are fresh,
sometimes a skiff of snow obscures the booted tracks,
but this I know—what we're building grows and grows,
with variants of tassled autumn leaves,
dirt brown now
a thready twig of bramble
an occasional beaver-chewed branch
one of us has hauled from the river's edge.

The rule, it seems, is never to cut or yank
growth from nearby vulnerable roots,
but to find a weighty stick that wants to join the others,
lying there, serene
alone against the snow,
fallen but waiting, wanting to become one of the many.

ෲ

II.

The distance of half a lifetime brings into focus the people of my past, the family members and loved ones whose own paths paralleled and intertwined with mine.

Air Space

Napping on the porch
faintly dreaming a jumbled childhood scene
I'm jolted by the scream of a Navy training jet high above me.
Hypnotized in four o'clock heat
I pretend I know close-up the pilot's face enveloped in his helmet:
sheen of skin, tensed lips, eyes locked and loaded with ambition.

Flying high maneuvers over me
navigating the curve of the earth
for my home he sees coordinates on geology
silver river threading through it
cliff shadows, and the texture of timber.

To bring him closer
I fancy in my unlikely reverie
he's descended from some grade school friend
seven decades and a thousand miles away.

Maybe he's the grandson of a young Rene? (anise cake and tears)
Or of Patricia? (eucalyptus leaves and dust)
Or Jimmy? (sweet alfalfa and moonlight)

His flight's contrail lingers like the smoke
of our long-ago grape leaf cigarettes
its dissipating echo like the thunder
on one hot June night when we huddled close with wonder.
How far away is the lightning?
Count the seconds.
Count the seconds.

Postwar Script

Rubber-banded, bundled, and boxed,
on silky onionskin and heavy weight Crane vellum
her letters were closeted for sixty years,
stacked by date,
until Mother's left-hand cursive lines,
her arrow-straight monotone,
unfolded from their confines into light.

One hundred letters to my father
gone first not far from New England but far enough
then gone for good to California

She was left with daughters
one a newborn, one already troubled
flat broke and back home again
with her own resentful mother's *I told you so* a daily slap
bore humility in the tall white house,
an edifice of propriety
on her hometown's tiny square.

Her letters to my father chronicled a husbandless life
of whooping cough, the tooth fairy, the tantrum,
the check you sent last month, shoes too small,
sign insurance papers, send birthday gifts, your mother called me
the doctor says rubella,
and
        When can you come back to visit?
        The girls both miss you.
        I will try to be a better wife.

Three years of Mother's letters
until one morning in winter 1949
with grandfather's money
she flew from Boston to San Francisco
        (propellers rumble above the clouds, two little red raincoats,
                      holiday lights on the tarmac)
to the new house and the old marriage
where nothing but their daughters ever fit just right again.

ಐಖಿ

Shirley Evelyn Lagsdin and her children.
Falmouth, Massachusetts, 1948.

Sisters

That reconciling year
(her daughter's wedding, my flight for it to Denver)
we learned our childhoods had few links
except for our quite unequal anguishes.

She, the elder, never knew
    that I once lied to the landlord, bold but terrified for both of us:
    Oh no, we never climbed in the fruit trees
    We never played in the haybarn's loft
    We never rode the horses bareback, galloping to the creek

And I, the younger, never knew
    that one night she left the house, joined a friend, met some boys
    and out in a pasture near Black Point Road
    was raped at knifepoint.

Five decades later, we are still
two girls separated not at birth
but by the life that happened after.

☙❧

Treasures

Only fifteen inches tall and not quite as wide,
my mother's Chinese chest of drawers
was a miniature even to me when I was little.

The orangey lacquered wood was carved in oriental intricacy
with veneer and trim and fretwork of glossy ginger brown
like four dragon's feet, thumb-sized legs below
and on top a tiny parapet like the low wall of a mandarin's terrace.

Its eight slim compartments were just big enough
for what she called her treasures:
her father's ivory edged harmonica
   a deck of playing cards for sleepless solitaire
      ballpoint pens from banks and tradesmen, rubber-banded
         a mass of thrift store bangles bought in haste
            and a pack of Camels hidden away from Daddy's disapproval.

Mother found it in a dusty San Francisco shop, summer 1953,
her only acquisition I know of that sprang from pure lust.
I imagine her trembling, eyeing it, looking away
then dollars unwillingly edged from the blue wallet
the shame of owning beauty when the bills are due.

The Chinese chest traveled to our different houses over decades
and rested briefly in a corner of her final tiny room
It has a loftier spot in my home now
but its drawers are still packed full
of Mother's timid spontaneity
her fears
her too few, too late indulgences.

Legacy

My mother's hands were square cut,
not clever or expressive but built for work.
Earlier, brown spotted with sun
later, red with poor circulation
her flat nails kept short, never with a glint of polish.

They were hands that would squash a buzzing wasp
in the corner of a windowsill
ferociously sandpaper an old dresser
and numb the startled wood to a helpless sheen.

They'd press, knuckles up, a tall sandwich to the plate,
cleave it with one swift slap of a blade
spade from the earth cylindrical plugs
and insert, swift and deep, a dozen tulip bulbs
scrub endlessly, angrily, with strong short bursts
our counters, floors and walls
grip a shoulder hard to steer me away from city traffic at the curb.

And mornings they'd tug into symmetrical submission every strand of
braid until my temples ached and then four times, the last with a
breathy dammit, crank the brown elastic band to hold it until bedtime.

The unsure times for my mother's hands
were the tremulous, hopeful press of red from a tube of Revlon,
the cautious peck of a number on the rotary phone
a frozen pose of glee punctuated
with a deathgrip on the stem of a party glass
her feathery pat on my father's back the relic of a hug.

In her last minutes, with the hospital's plastic wristband a bracelet
she never would have worn
her hand hesitated, sought my own and transferred what it could
of her cold unerring strength.

☙❧

Vigil

The gurgle of oxygenated water
Over the narrow-gauge white bed
Muffles the rattle and hum of hallway business
(A cough, squeaking shoes, glasses on a tray, bantered greetings)
And Mother's bird-narrow chest moves at heartbeat speed
To push and pull at air she cannot use.

*I once captured with intent to save
A hummingbird at my inside windowsill
My cupped hands curled around it
And I walked swiftly to the porch
To let it jet off—frantic.
I forgot to look at it close
For the first and last time in my hands.
I only knew by books its fragile iridescence
And books are not the way to know a bird.*

Silver April drizzle mutes the courtyard colors past the window glass.
Pristine, well-bleached hygienics render scent inert.

The saline bag's gone down from "10" to "7."
We've agreed at "1" not to replenish it.
So Mother's smooth dark skin will cool
The veins collapse with dryness
And oxygen will be redundant.

*To hold a bird one second
And to glimpse it flying into the willows
Is knowledge enough for a lifetime.*

ଓଃ଼ଠ

Floating

Mother's ashes mingle and float
Not dissolving but drifting
Guiding each other in a dim cloud
To rocks shimmering below the water's surface
Moving with the ocean's pulse
Toward the low fringe of surf reaching softly for the beach.

Duty done, I step into the water and float alone.
From chin to jowl to hairline
The wimple and cowl of dark Atlantic water frames my face
Tight cool silk in a perfect oblong of ordination.

My eyes closed as if in prayer
I face the fire of eleven o'clock sun
Resisting verticality
Suspended by faith
Buoyant in joy
With breasts and hips half-hidden in deep water
Arms outstretched, compliant daughter
A full sacrament among the random strands of seaweed.

Through vagaries of water I hear
the harmonic hum of distant laughter
Muffled sea boats farther out
And the low fringe of surf
reaching softly for the blessed beach.

ॐ

Childless

My decision, not ever made,
was never unmade.
Like a perennially rumpled bed,
to daily smooth and tuck betrays intention
it lingered,
firmed itself with repetition and attrition
became a commonplace fact
natural as breathing
or not holding my breath
endured three decades' rhetoric, sans tact:
   fulfillment   a woman's place   a mother's love   the ticking clock
and made a protocol of its own:
   the non-plan   the won't happen   the can't have   the never goal

Long past the lump of coal in my throat
at merry-go-rounds and Christmas plays
photo albums, small shoes, and penciled heights on doorways
my decision became
              (natural as rain flies south and birds fall up)
the *I have chosen.*

☙❧

When I Try

(in the manner of Nikki Giovanni)

when I try too hard to love you
i trip and stutter   not my best mode
i can feel the blush begin
and my heart's a crazy drum

when i try too hard to love you
my words are fluff
or rice crispy insignificant
too light   too sassy   too glib

when i try too hard to love you
     beautiful you
the not-so-beautiful me
feels only half as fine
reflected in your dark eyes

so   when you try too hard to love me
maybe i'll remember how it feels
maybe i'll see myself again in
your blush   heart   words   eyes

and i will be kinder than you

☙❧

I've Never Asked

I've never asked too much of you
Or cried out in my anger
The tears I've cried have been too few
A broken vase, a life askew
The presence of a stranger

But promises are way past due
And I sense a looming danger

The tears I've cried have been too few

I'll tell you love and tell you true
And on my life I'll wager
I've never asked too much of you
With no regrets for what I'll do
I'm thriving on my rage here

I've never asked enough of you
and the tears we've cried have been too few

൙൞

Cuppa

Morning alarm rattles the warmth
In the mile-away kitchen milk foam whisks in a pan
And my comforter is here with coffee
Joins the sleepy tangle
On the flanneled mattress
Of paper   dog   sunbeam   mug   bedrumpled head

True romance
That love, these mornings
Just my cup of tea

Road Trip

Conversation's richer in the car.
Facing the same direction
locks us in benign inattention
to anything but ourselves
the muffled sound of time passing
and the landscape of our movement.

Driving together, we understand the distances
having weathered some together in this lifetime
and the tricky slope of a once familiar road.

ಚ೮

Call and Response

"I'm all right!" I shout from the kitchen
The clang of the dropped kettle still ringing
food askew on the tiled floor
"OK!" he calls down from the upstairs office

The distance between the clang and my shout is forever
The distance between the clang and my shout is his prayer

o god let life go on   in this house   precisely as it was last minute

My call of reassurance comes quicker
than "Come down here!" would—
If I take a tumble on the step, say
or slice through my thumb:
Am I hurt? Am I harmed?
Self-consciousness precedes it

"I'm all right!" carries confidence
Holds more authority
than any plea for help

"I'm all right!" is the pure and sudden love
of being loved
and needs no introduction

It's his quick prayer in reverse

෧෮

You Fill Me

for my mate Mike, the chef

You're the first big sip of Maker's Mark
And Coke on the porch along about dark
The click of my spoon on the crème brulee.

You're turkey gravy on leftover stuffin'
You're the top of the muffin.
You're a butter-soft, thumb-high filet mignon
You're crab chunks buried in the court-bouillon
You're strong hot coffee in a weak cold dawn.

You're shrimp and grits with a side of greens
And a half-shell oyster on a crisp Saltine
You're pecan banana bread with chocolate chips
You're the first good strawberry on my lips

You're the childhood kitchen of a grown-up dream
You stir my saucepan, you spice my bowl
You fill the tummy of my soul.

☙❧

III.

The commentary in my head has crept unbidden onto the page at irregular intervals. An essay, a blog, a story about daily life wasn't quite the right medium. Poetry was the better outlet.

Patio, Circa 1955

Walking across the patio on a dark night
You're secure with the glow of the kitchen door behind you
Shooting its long wedge of pale gold on the dusty flagstones.
With homeglow as escort and ally
You're totally safe on the journey out—
A simple child's task
Emptying the garbage, say, or taking a tool to the neighbors.

It's the coming back that takes your breath away.

The scented bay trees, mumbling creek and deep woods
Are no longer the friends you knew in daylight
So you've learned to clench your fear like a fist
Walk slow and sure
Softly whistling
Thinking only of the house, coffee ice cream,
Warm pajamas and a Nancy Drew book.

Braver, with back tingling
Eyes focused on the distant glowing doorway
You move toward home, away from the night

Behind, above, at your back is a vast black pool
Of everything you can't describe or take the blame for
And ahead shines only a thin gold slit of welcoming light to aim for.

Years later, reconciled to coming and going in the dark
You wonder this:
Shouldn't venturing out into the world be fraught with terror
And coming into the house again pure bliss?

ぐる

Learning the Waters

Mine was the old school.
Not like this where ideas are whirlpools,
flashfloods, deluges and diversion ditches.

No, it was old school, where facts came steadily out the tap
and filled the clean container
and the tap-tap-tap of high heels
on hard linoleum kept cadence
with the intravenous drip of how it's always been.

The pool of learning was very still there
unrippled by contention, upheld by convention
sturdy desks in straight lines facing Him or Her.

Sixty years later I do math in my head, fast.
I can say the who-what-when-where-why of European wars
and write the six Greek metric feet in poetry.
Mutation, thermocline, cumulus, photosynthesis—I've got it down,
and how the Romans built their towns.
I know axon and dendrite, agape and eros,
Dickens, Dickinson, Dinesen, cubits and furlongs,
Cancer and Capricorn, lee and windward.

But I learned from the shore or anchored in familiar harbors
I would not have dared to navigate your frigid roiling waters
push myself headlong into waves of vast uncertainty
or search submerged without a map for sunken treasure.

Mine was the old school—
still waters, a known course, smooth sailing.

☙❧

Three Cheers for Fears

The pulse of primal fears kept our newborn species safe from danger.
Hardwired to shiver and leap, their hearts pumped adrenaline
the ancestral dread deep in their DNA
    of dark shapes looming in the ocean
    a sudden clatter of rattle in the brush
    the thunder of rapids ahead on a placid river.

This millennia too we're alert to the hazards in the world:
    The scream of too-late brakes before the grind of metal
    The shout, the clatter of glass and sudden hush of bar fight
    A uniformed stranger on the doorstep, hat in hand.

Words too can bring that sudden chill, that zero at the bone.
"I'm sorry, we show no record of that transaction"
    "You've been a great asset to the company"
        "The doctor would like to talk to you in person"
And "Honey, I need to tell you something important."

Soft and civilized, with indolent habits of mind
and sedentary luxuries
we need, some days, the electric jolt
of a nameless fear of nature:
wildfire, or steam from the side of a mountain
that makes us one again
with wary tigers, mammoths, snakes
and other less complacent beings.

☙❧

Old Ways and Nowadays

In the old days of cowpunchers and roundups,
long hours of riding the range,
every horse was run hard in the toughest terrain,
and no one considered it strange.
A cayuse from the outfit's remuda
was saddled up with a cowpoke's own tack—
every bridle as good as the next one,
any rigging fit each horse's back.

A dive down a coulee at the end of a rope
on the horns of a two-year old steer
was a pretty good lesson in *speed-up* and *turn*,
with a few granite boulders to clear.
The sudden approach of a cliff at a lope
was the place to learn *sit down* and *whoa*
and no horse that was fit and got fed every day
got to choose to just stop… or not go.

Oh, these days a horseman might gaze at the hills
as he unties his horse from the rail,
but chances are good he'll just stay in the 'hood
and never set foot on a trail.
No, he'll head for the covered arena,
where the footing is synthetic sand,
and the obstacles there aren't cactus and rock
but PVC poles placed by hand.

He's tried snaffles and curbs, a modified pelham,
a hackamore rig and a spade,
and his reins went from lined, to soft nylon cord,
to Mexican leather in braid.
A computer-fit saddle for him and his horse
is built by a comp'ny back east
and his blanket's all wool with a microflex core,
sheer comfort for man and for beast.

His schedule each day—an hour at most—
means some work on the most basic moves:
hips over, flexation, round circles, both leads
and a slide that leaves parallel grooves.
Bell boots on the horse keep her safe all around
(with leggings and aluminum shoes)
and a three-minute break after trotting the fence
her reward for remembering cues.

But who'll say that an old-time cowpuncher
with a hell-bent-for-leather agenda
didn't dote on his favorite old paint from the herd
with petting and words whispered tender?

Does the modern-day cowboy with a Wrangler ensemble
and boots that are shiny, not battered,
sometimes yearn for the days when a man and his horse
were a team—with a real job that mattered?

CR&O

I. Dreams of Dude String Horses: On the Picket Line

"I'd choose that little red-haired girl—she's funny and she's cute
With freckles dancing on her nose and tassels on her boots."

    "I've got my eye on the chubby kid, his name I think is Sam
    Who swaggers right up close to the fence as happy as a clam."

"I like the grandma with the cowboy hat and the dusty denim jeans
Quieter than most, she doesn't boast; been riding since her teens."

    "Those twin girls have long blond bangs, forelocks just like mine
    They take their time to give a pat to the horses on the line."

"The best of them is the older guy who scratches my neck where I like
He scans my legs and checks for rocks as he lifts each hoof just right
Then loosens the strap on my old curb bit and pulls the cinch up tight.

"He swings so light in the saddle I can hardly feel his weight
With a subtle nudge and a soft 'Go, pal' we move out at four-beat gait
Not a shuffle but a real trail walk, then we're trotting fast and straight.

"His legs are still, the reins hang loose, he's centered on my back
With him I'm more than a dude string horse, gentle and easy to pack.

"When we ride out on those special days, it takes me way, way back:
I'm a blue-blood winner, a Lipizzan stallion, Man O'War and The Black."

☙❧

II. Dreams of Dude String Horses: The Old Campaigner

I spent my youth as a cutting horse.
Strong and plenty fast
I'd spin and swerve and fake that cow
and then put on the gas.
But too much stop and too much turn
have wrecked my aging hips
so I gave up stands filled with shouting fans,
no more long trailer trips.

Now I amble slow with my precious load,
and yet it never fails
that once a summer (maybe less)
I hear those mournful wails,
and I have to stop and wait for pop
or the wrangler who's trying
to whoa the group, ride down the line
and rescue whoever's crying.

As slow and sure as I can be,
that youngster's filled with fears;
my height, my bulk, the thought of me,
brings her to anxious tears.
I've done no wrong, no one's been hurt,
but in my heart I know
she's scared. Of me? A gentleman—
a trophied, purebred pro!

If I could advise each tearful child
who's still in my memory
I'd tell each one of the years of fun,
the trails, the arenas and galloping free
that they could savor (if they'd just be braver)
riding a horse as good as me.

CR₂O

Insomnia

One o'clock. Night sweats, nightmares, times a-wasting, no one cares
star struck, moonblind, I play alphabet to smooth my tangled mind
from Agincourt to Zenda (lit locales), Arnst to Zamorra (teenage pals)
I wonder if there really is a heaven? The digital truth is three-o-seven.

I slog at a run through deep detritus
(we're your brain cells, do not fight us)
ancient slights, and wish-I'd-saids
wallpaper over childhood beds
the words to a favorite Broadway tune
did I start retirement way too soon?
Sheets a-tangle, pillow's mashed, all my hopes for sleep are dashed.

That poem I lost from a first-time writer
a surprisingly guilt free one-nighter
the leg that shattered under my horse
and whether to take a Spanish course
upcoming deadlines, family troubles
they all collide like backyard bubbles.
I form Jeopardy answers: every clue, five whole categories all in blue.

Bad decisions, better choices, the cars I've owned and distant voices
Four-and-twenty meets my eyes, blackbirds flock from blackbird pies
Eight full hours? Not a chance. I'm partnering a crazy mental dance…
Breath's uneven, eyes are burning, I'm flopping, redirecting, churning.

I hear the poodle's breathy snore from his pillow on the floor
and my mate exhales with regularity, unaware of our vast disparity.
In syncopation I hear their rhythm—
I want to be there, sleeping, with 'em.

☙

The Big Z

Disregard them when they're teeny
and risk a jungle of zucchini.
Just turn your head and—oh my gosh!
A bumper crop of camo-squash.
With sneaky runners under cover
and tendrils prone to grab and smother
crowding peppers, broccoli, lettuce
could it be they're out to get us?

The stuff will thrive in rocks and silt
and gardeners can't live with guilt
it's never yams or pears or parsnips—
it's zukes the neighbors leave on doorsteps.
So lock your vehicle when you go driving,
somewhere nearby a plant is thriving.
If you park for a while and wander far
expect zucchinis in your car.

☙❧

Everybeach

From Bolinas to Vernazza
Falmouth to Point Reyes
each swimming beach of mine
from then to now
becomes one beach in memory.

Arms held subtly in a highwire balance
I storkwalk into the shallows
and resolve at just-so-cold to plunge under
accept the sudden chosen doom of dark water.

The first two minutes out on shore
flopped horizontal, breathing hard
the known world becomes
towel dented into sand by thighs and torso
the warm animal scent of my own golden arms
and in ears still bubbling from submersion
the keening underwater sound of distant laughter
meets the thudding swat of boats veering close.

Aching, body core cold against the sun
I will its rays to sear me too hot
to force one more exquisite moment
of surrender to the water.

Each memory beach from then to now
an internal compromise:
the icy certainty of venturing
against the delicious warmth of return.

೦೩೮೦

Georgia on My Mind

There, around the museum corner,
like a sudden soundless waterfall
or the first right turn into the Academy
where the statue of David grabs your breath
and holds it captive
stands a faceless dressmaker's form
shrined by velvet ropes.

The diminutive mannequin
wears her last rusty black garment:
cotton, a wrap cinched in silver conchos,
sleeves to the wrist,
white silk at the high throat.
On surrounding walls,
glowing in the soft light
and the still cool air of the gallery
skulls and dry arroyos, virginal waiting blooms
and lusty, wanton, full-petaled irises
still radiate O'Keefe's own desert heat.

Hey! Don't ever try to tell me

That I need to test this product on another part of the garment
That I have to write my address and account number on the envelope
That I have to wait one full minute before I rinse out that conditioner
That if I don't put up the little flag, they won't take my letter
when they leave the mail
That rectal bleeding, ulcers, tinnitus and suicide ideation
are acceptable side effects of anything

And don't ever tell me
That this can of wasp spray won't kill that line of ants
That I can't use a fork to dislodge that bread in my toaster
That a slobbery good morning kiss from my dog is toxic
That a 70-year-old woman held hostage for a month
wants a phone call and a hot meal first
not a mirror and tweezers

If you think I believe you, then you believe that:
Nobody dog ears a library book to save their place
20 percent of the total is what the waitress gets, every time
We all merge smoothly in the order of our arrival at the roundabout
Baked Brussels sprouts is a more ennobling entrée than rare prime rib
And that a vintage wife never indulges in a little checkout-stand banter
with a flirtable man

Don't tell me that! I don't believe you.

⋈

Metrical

A child's spondees are
Sun   Beach   Dog   Soup   Bath   Sleep   Laugh   Ouch   Kiss

Then come the years of trochees:
COLLege   WEDDing
WORKload   MORTgage
CHILDbirth   FAMily
HOUSEhold   BUDget

                              (and an iamb: diVORCE)

The dactyls of middle age:
HOLiday   and   CATalogue
TENure track   and   DIVidend
EXercise   and   SUMmerplace

Twin dactyls chime in strong eventually:
 REGular MAMMograms
      CATaract SURgery
           GRANDkid in GUESTroom
                CARDioVAScular
                      DOUBle inDEMnity

In later years we'll come to know the quads:
ANGiogram   MELenoma   inCONtinence   conTINgency   exECutor
And in the end, again those simple little onesomes:

                                          Life

                                          Love

                                          Death

                             ෂ෮

No eating no dogs

(hand-lettered sign on a minimarket door)

Protect me from my foolish self,
and deliver me from litigation.
Give me the weight limit of this shelf,
post "highly flammable" at each gas station.
List the additives in my tonic,
tell me where the road gets narrow.
Warn me of deafness stereophonic
and con-men who would drain my marrow
and fleas that carry plague bubonic,
and rabies from that backyard sparrow.

If hantavirus comes from mice
and stomach cancer from too much spice
and air bags can crush a pre-teenager
and the midday sun's a deadly wager—
then as sure as drugs killed John Belushi,
we'll die from toxins in the sushi.
If fluorescent bulbs can't be stared into
and if asbestos haunts that cute new rental
I'll need a manual (or a lucky charm)
to help me function safe from harm.

Undercooked eggs and too hot coffee are
just as ruthless as the Mafia,
so let me know some foods acceptable
in a place the government's deemed impeccable.

Alert me when there's too much smog
to exercise my little dog,
the one with dander that brings on allergies
like paint fumes in unvented galleries.

Post the signs and raise the awareness
from tornadoes to perms that could leave us hairless.
The world, it seems, is always with us.

For foolhardy choices—please forgive us.

෴

My Heaven

My heaven will have a lost-and-found
a rack with favorite hats and gloves I thought were gone forever.

And weather:
soft rain, hard wind, deep snow, breezes over muddy ground
hot drooping afternoons with pools of shade.

My heaven will have a tall poodle to nap, long legs akimbo,
and to press his head unbidden against my knee

And books for faithless me,
each a brand-new love
plucked eagerly off the shelf
after I've finished the last, remorseless.

My heaven will have green pastures for the horses,
my lucky lifetime eight
grazing just past the pearly gates

And water.
I'll wade fast into rivers and lakes,
then take the sudden deep dive
relishing one more minute of every sense alive.

In that someday heaven
I'll thank my lucky stars (in constellations I can't recite)
watch a mountain sunset with its glow unending
and hope for a skyful of northern lights,
a shimmering cosmic ladder
for the next person's easy ascending.

౦౩౯౦

Acknowledgments

The following poems have been previously published in various editions of *The Shrub-Steppe Poetry Journal*.
    Western Dream: A True Life Real Estate Saga
    Real. Pretty.
    Methow Wind
    Terra Firma Eastside
    At The Dalles
    Habitat I: Renewal
    Habitat II: Reminder
    Air Space
    Postwar Script
    Sisters
    Legacy
    Insomnia
    Everybeach
    Georgia On My Mind

The following poems have been previously published by Yakima Coffeehouse Poets.
    In Country
    Childless
    Habitat I: Renewal

About the Author

Susan Lagsdin encouraged many young poets during her career as a teacher of writing. She also captured her own memories and perceptions in verse and, in this volume, has collected her favorites—some published, many performed—from five decades of writing.

Born in New England and raised in California's Bay Area, Susan has spent most of her adult years in the inland Northwest. She's said that her earliest roots grew and held fast in the Methow Valley, where she launched her teaching career, directed community theater productions, and rode horseback on mountain trails. Since 2006, she's lived in East Wenatchee with journalist and photographer Mike Irwin.

Susan taught English at Wenatchee Valley College and is on the board of directors of Write on the River. She is currently a member of Confluence Poets, reads at Shrub-Steppe Poetry open mics, and writes and edits articles for a handful of regional publications.

Colophon

Never Again That Simple, by Susan Lagsdin,
was set in Calibri by Methow Press.
Title font Eras Demi ITC.
The cover design is by Greg Wright.
The cover and interior images are by Mike Irwin.
The photo on page 28 was provided by the author.
Manufactured by LightningSource, LaVergne, Tennessee.